The Little Book of Quotes by Women

ISBN-13: 978-0983918233

The Little Book of Quotes by Women

Inspiring Words to Live By

Edited by
Kathleen Welton

The Little Quote Books Series

Table of Contents

Thank You
Introduction

Biographical Index
About the Editor

Thank You

With gratitude to all of the women who have left their stamp on history and to those women who are currently leaving their stamp on our lives little by little—by recording their classic, simple, and inspiring words to live by.

Introduction

This book is a collection of quotes from the women who have appeared on U.S. postage stamps. The women featured in this book are activists, actors, athletes, artists, attorneys, authors, choreographers, comedians, dancers, designers, engineers, First Ladies, journalists, mothers, musicians, nurses, Olympians, painters, physicians, pilots, poets, publishers, Queens, scientists, senators, singers, wives, writers, and more. And they all share one thing in common. These women have indeed left their stamp on history.

The world's first adhesive postage stamp also known as Penny Black was issued nearly 175 years ago in Britain in May 1840. It featured a woman—Queen Victoria who is also known as saying *"The important thing is not what they think of me, but what I think of them."*

Penny Black/Issued 1840

In July 1847, the U.S. issued is first adhesive postage stamps featuring stamps of both Benjamin Franklin and George Washington. The first U.S. postage stamp featuring a woman appeared in January 1893 with Queen Isabella of Castile from Spain in honor of her patronage to making the trips of Christopher Columbus to the New World possible.

Queen Isabella I/Columbus Announcing His Discovery/Issued 1893

The first U.S. postage stamp featuring an American woman appeared in December 1902 with the portrait of Martha Washington.

Martha Washington/Issued 1902

Beginning in 1902 and now for more than 100 years, there are more than 200 U.S. postage stamps that commemorate both women and women's issues.

This book contains 365 quotes from more than 100 of the women that have appeared on U.S. postage stamps over these years. The quotes in this book have been organized to cover a dozen topics that will hopefully provide inspiration—a quote to use for each day of the year.

The quotes are arranged alphabetically by each author in each section so that you can easily find your favorites.

The quotes are arranged for easy access in each section on topics as follows:

✻ Beauty
✻ Courage
✻ Freedom
✻ Friendship
✻ Happiness
✻ Lessons
✻ Life
✻ Love
✻ Possibility
✻ Service
✻ Strength
✻ Work

I have been an avid collector of both quotes and postage stamps as long as I can remember. The idea for this book took hold when I was gathering additional favorite quotes by women for a new book. I wanted to provide a unique book that would tell a compelling story.

So here it is…a book of favorite quotes by women who were also featured on U.S. postage stamps.

While I was familiar with many of these women and their quotes, I enjoyed discovering even more inspirational quotes by them as well as new quotes from other women.

There are numerous biographies and other resources of particular interest on the subject of women on U.S. postage stamps including the book *Women on United States Postage Stamps* by Anita Price Davis and Louise Hunt and the exhibit "Women in the Postal Service and Philately" from the Smithsonian National Postal Museum.

My hope is that you will enjoy this book and the selection of both the women and their quotes.

May you think highly of them.

Enjoy,
Kathleen Welton
August 2014

Beauty

Louisa May Alcott/Issued 1940

Far away there in the sunshine are my highest aspirations.
I may not reach them, but I can look up and see their beauty,
believe in them, and try to follow where they lead.
~Louisa May Alcott

When I sing, I don't want them to see that my face is black.
I don't want them to see that my face is white.
I want them to see my soul. And that is colorless.
~Marian Anderson

We ask justice, we ask equality, we ask that all the civil and
political rights that belong to citizens of the United States,
be guaranteed to us and our daughters forever.
~Susan B. Anthony

Give light and people will find the way.
~Ella Baker

O beautiful for spacious skies,
For amber waves of grain,
For purple mountain majesties
Above the fruited plain!
America! America! God shed His grace on thee,
And crown thy good with brotherhood
From sea to shining sea!
~Katherine Lee Bates

❧

Those who contemplate the beauty of the earth find reserves
of strength that will endure as long as life lasts. There is
something infinitely healing in the repeated refrains of nature—
the assurance that dawn comes after night,
and spring after winter.
~Rachel Carson

❧

Which of my photographs is my favorite? The one I'm going
to take tomorrow.
~Imogen Cunningham

❧

Dance in the body you have.
~Agnes de Mille

❧

Beauty

Beauty—be not caused—It Is—
Chase it, and it ceases—
Chase it not, and it abides—
~Emily Dickinson

Truth is such a rare thing, it is delightful to tell it.
~Emily Dickinson

By Chivalries as tiny,
A Blossom, or a Book,
The seeds of smiles are planted—
Which blossom in the dark.
~Emily Dickinson

༄

After midnight, the moon set, I was alone with the stars. I have often said that the lure of flying is the lure of beauty, and I need no other flight to convince me that the reason flyers fly, whether they know it or not, is the esthetic appeal of flying.
~Amelia Earhart

༄

Nobody cares
if you can't dance well.
Just get up and dance.
Great dancers are not great
because of their technique,
they are great because of
their PASSION.
~Martha Graham

༄

The beauty of a woman is not in a facial mode but the true beauty in a woman is reflected in her soul. It is the caring that she lovingly gives the passion that she shows. The beauty of a woman grows with the passing years.

~Audrey Hepburn

꩜

The best and most beautiful things in the world cannot be seen or even touched—they must be felt with the heart.

~Helen Keller

꩜

Beauty is whatever gives joy.

~Edna St. Vincent Millay

꩜

Beauty is everlasting.

~Marianne Moore

꩜

We too often bind ourselves by authorities rather than by the truth.

~Lucretia Mott

꩜

Beauty is only skin deep, but ugly goes clean to the bone.

~Dorothy Parker

꩜

Beauty

Manners are a sensitive awareness of the feelings of others.
If you have that awareness, you have good manners,
no matter what fork you use.
~Emily Post

⟡

It isn't enough to talk about peace. One must believe in it. And it
isn't enough to believe in it. One must work at it.
~Eleanor Roosevelt

No matter how plain a woman may be, if truth and honesty are
written across her face, she will be beautiful.
~Eleanor Roosevelt

Beautiful young people are accidents of nature, but beautiful old
people are works of art.
~Eleanor Roosevelt

The future belongs to those who believe in the beauty
of their dreams.
~Eleanor Roosevelt

⟡

Never underestimate the power of dreams and the influence
of the human spirit. We are all the same in this notion:
The potential for greatness lives within each of us.
~Wilma Rudolph

⟡

The past, the present and the future are really one:
they are today.

~Harriet Beecher Stowe

So much has been said and sung of beautiful young girls, why
doesn't somebody wake up to the beauty of old women?

~Harriet Beecher Stowe

Life is an opportunity, benefit from it.
Life is beauty, admire it.
Life is a dream, realize it.
Life is a challenge, meet it.
Life is a duty, complete it.
Life is a game, play it.
Life is a promise, fulfill it.
Life is sorrow, overcome it.
Life is a song, sing it.
Life is a struggle, accept it.
Life is a tragedy, confront it.
Life is an adventure, dare it.
Life is luck, make it.
Life is too precious, do not destroy it.
Life is life, fight for it.

~Mother Teresa

It is a kingly act to assist the fallen.

~Mother Teresa

Every great dream begins with a dreamer. Always remember, you have within you the strength, the patience, and the passion to reach for the stars to change the world.

~Harriet Tubman

There are two ways of spreading light. To be the candle, or the mirror that reflects it.

~Edith Wharton

Courage

Amelia Earhart/Issued 1963

No man or woman who tries to pursue an ideal in his or her own
way is without enemies.
~Daisy Gatson Bates

The art of losing isn't hard to master;
so many things seem filled with the intent
to be lost that their loss is no disaster.
~Elizabeth Bishop

It is not easy to be a pioneer—but oh, it is fascinating!
I would not trade one moment, even the worst moment,
for all the riches in the world.
~Elizabeth Blackwell

Let the world know you as you are, not as you think you
should be, because sooner or later, if you are posing, you will
forget the pose, and then where are you?
~Fanny Brice

❧

The most difficult thing is the decision to act,
the rest is merely tenacity.
~Amelia Earhart

Courage is the price that life exacts for granting peace.
~Amelia Earhart

❧

The only way I can pay back for what fate and society
have handed me is to try, in minor totally useless ways,
to make an angry sound against injustice.
~Martha Gellhorn

❧

I think that little by little I'll be able to solve
my problems and survive.
~Frida Kahlo

❧

The key to artistic photography is to work out your own
thoughts, by yourselves. Imitation leads to certain disaster.
~Gertrude Käsebier

❧

Character cannot be developed in ease and quiet. Only through experience of trial and suffering can the soul be strengthened, vision cleared, ambition inspired, and success achieved.
~Helen Keller

Never bend your head, always hold it high. Look the world straight in the face.
~Helen Keller

❦

You have come to the shore. There are no instructions.
~Denise Levertov

❦

The glory of each generation is to make its own precedents.
~Belva Ann Lockwood

❦

Right is right, even if no one else does it.
~Juliette Gordon Low

❦

Don't shoot until you see the whites of their eyes.
~Sybil Ludington

❦

If you know you are on the right track, if you have this
inner knowledge, then nobody can turn you off...
no matter what they say.
~*Barbara McClintock*

ᕤᕫ

Not truth, but faith, it is that keeps the world alive.
~*Edna St. Vincent Millay*

ᕤᕫ

With enough courage, you can do without a reputation.
~*Margaret Mitchell*

ᕤᕫ

If I hadn't started painting, I would have raised chickens.
~*Grandma Moses*

ᕤᕫ

To create one's world in any of the arts takes courage.
~*Georgia O'Keeffe*

ᕤᕫ

I have learned over the years that when one's mind is made up,
this diminishes fear.
~*Rosa Parks*

ᕤᕫ

Why do they always teach us that it's easy and evil to do what
we want and that we need discipline to restrain ourselves? It's
the hardest thing in the world—to do what we want. And it takes
the greatest kind of courage. I mean, what we really want.
~Ayn Rand

☙

Do what you feel in your heart to be right—for you'll be
criticized anyway. You'll be damned if you do, and damned if
you don't.
~Eleanor Roosevelt

You gain strength, courage, and confidence by every experience
in which you really stop to look fear in the face...You must do
the thing you think you cannot do.
~Eleanor Roosevelt

It takes courage to love, but pain through love is the purifying
fire which those who love generously know. We all know people
who are so much afraid of pain that they shut themselves up like
clams in a shell and, giving out nothing, receive nothing and
therefore shrink until life is a mere living death.
~Eleanor Roosevelt

What we need in the world is manners...I think that if, instead of
preaching brotherly love, we preached good manners, we might
get a little further. It sounds less righteous and more practical.
~Eleanor Roosevelt

It is better to light a candle than curse the darkness.
~Eleanor Roosevelt

The moment we begin to fear the opinions of others
and hesitate to tell the truth that is in us, and from motives
of policy are silent when we should speak,
the divine floods of light and life no longer
flow into our souls.
~Elizabeth Cady Stanton

Freedom

Betsy Ross/Issued 1952

In the unceasing ebb and flow of justice and oppression
we must all dig channels as best we may, that at the propitious
moment somewhat of the swelling tide may be conducted to the
barren places of life.
~Jane Addams

True peace is not merely the absence of war,
it is the presence of justice.
~Jane Addams

I think knowing what you cannot do is more important than
knowing what you can do. In fact, that's good taste.
~Lucille Ball

The secret of staying young is to live honestly, eat slowly, and
lie about your age.
~Lucille Ball

None who have always been free can understand the terrible
fascinating power of the hope of freedom to those who are not
free.
~Pearl S. Buck

༺

Movements are as eloquent as words.
~Isadora Duncan

If I could tell you want it meant, there would no point in dancing
it.
~Isadora Duncan

༺

If you want to change attitudes, start with a change in behavior.
~Katharine Hepburn

I never lose sight of the fact that just being is fun.
~Katharine Hepburn

If you always do what interests you, at least one person is
pleased.
~Katharine Hepburn

༺

Women who stepped up were measured as
citizens of the nation, not as women...this was a people's war,
and everyone was in it.
~Oveta Culp Hobby

The rule of thumb is a simple one. Regard each man, each woman, as an individual, not as a Catholic, a Protestant, or a Jew; not as an Indian, American, or European. Like or dislike a person for his own intrinsic qualities—not because he belongs to a different race or subscribes to a different religion.

Dignify man with individuality.

~Oveta Culp Hobby

People don't understand the kind of fight it takes to record what you want to record the way you want to record it.

~Billie Holiday

If I'm going to sing like someone else,
then I don't need to sing at all.

~Billie Holiday

You can't copy anybody and end with anything. If you copy, it means you're working without any real feeling. No two people on earth are alike, and it's got to be that way in music or it isn't music.

~Billie Holiday

I will assume the undertaking for my own crown of Castile, and am ready to pawn my jewels to defray the expenses of it, if the funds in the treasury should be found inadequate.

~Isabella I of Castile

The clash of ideas is the sound of freedom.
~*Lady Bird Johnson*

❧

Getting angry doesn't solve anything.
~*Grace Kelly*

❧

The work of today is the history of tomorrow,
and we are its makers.
~*Juliette Gordon Low*

❧

When you choose your fields of labor go where nobody else
is willing to go.
~*Mary Lyon*

❧

It is one of my sources of happiness never to desire a knowledge
of other people's business.
~*Dolley Madison*

❧

Every component of the organism is as much of an organism as
every other part.
~*Barbara McClintock*

❧

Freedom

Never doubt that a small group of thoughtful,
committed citizens can change the world.
Indeed, it is the only thing that ever has.
~Margaret Mead

∽

I believe that everything happens for a reason.
People change so that you can learn to let go,
things go wrong so that you appreciate them when they're right,
you believe lies so you eventually learn to trust no one
but yourself, and sometimes good things fall apart
so better things can fall together.
~Marilyn Monroe

I'm not interested in money, I just want to be wonderful.
~Marilyn Monroe

∽

You must create your own world. I am responsible for my
world.
~Louise Nevelson

∽

I would like to be known as a person who is concerned about
freedom and equality and justice and prosperity for all people.
~Rosa Parks

∽

I never doubted that equal rights was the right direction.
Most reforms, most problems are complicated.
But to me there is nothing complicated
about ordinary equality.
~Alice Paul

Freedom (n.): To ask nothing. To expect nothing.
To depend on nothing.
~Ayn Rand

Sometimes I wonder if we shall ever grow up in our politics and
say definite things which mean something, or whether we shall
always go on using generalities to which everyone can
subscribe, and which mean very little.
~Eleanor Roosevelt

Today the American knight holds the commercial supremacy of
the world.
~Betsy Ross

Friendship

Eleanor Roosevelt/Issued 1963

One of the things I learned the hard way was that it doesn't pay
to get discouraged. Keeping busy and making optimism
a way of life can restore your faith in yourself.
~Lucille Ball

I have an everyday religion that works for me.
Love yourself first, and everything else falls into line.
You really have to love yourself
to get anything done in this world.
~Lucille Ball

The best time to make friends is before you need them.
~Ethel Barrymore

I love people. I love my family, my children…but inside myself is a place where I live all alone and that's where you renew your springs that never dry up.
~*Pearl S. Buck*

You cannot make yourself feel something you do not feel, but you can make yourself do right in spite of your feelings.
~*Pearl S. Buck*

There is no Frigate like a Book
To take us Lands away
Nor any Coursers like a Page
Of Prancing Poetry —
~*Emily Dickinson*

The Soul selects her own Society —
Then — shuts the Door —
To her divine Majority —
Present no more —
~*Emily Dickinson*

"Hope" is the thing with feathers —
That perches in the soul —
And sings the tune without the words —
And never stops — at all —
~*Emily Dickinson*

Friendship

If you need a helping hand, you can find one
at the end of your arm.
~Katharine Hepburn

❦

If I don't have friends, then I ain't got nothin'.
~Billie Holiday

Sometimes it's worse to win a fight than to lose.
~Billie Holiday

❦

I would rather walk with a friend in the dark, than alone in the
light.
~Helen Keller

❦

Ours is a circle of friendships united by ideals.
~Juliette Gordon Low

❦

We all respect sincerity in our friends and acquaintances,
but Hollywood is willing to pay for it.
~Hattie McDaniel

❦

My candle burns at both ends;
It will not last the night;
But ah, my foes, and oh, my friends —
It gives a lovely light!
~Edna St. Vincent Millay

ॐ

The smallest minority on earth is the individual. Those who deny individual rights cannot claim to be defenders of minorities.
~Ayn Rand

ॐ

Friendship with oneself is all-important, because without it one cannot be friends with anyone else in the world.
~Eleanor Roosevelt

A little simplification would be the first step toward rational living, I think.
~Eleanor Roosevelt

ॐ

Friendships are discovered rather than made.
~Harriet Beecher Stowe

Common sense is seeing things as they are; and doing things as they ought to be.
~Harriet Beecher Stowe

The truth is the kindest thing we can give folks in the end.
~Harriet Beecher Stowe

The bitterest tears shed over graves are for words left unsaid and deeds left undone.
~Harriet Beecher Stowe

I did not write it. God wrote it. I merely did his dictation.
~Harriet Beecher Stowe

It's a matter of taking the side of the weak against the strong, something the best people have always done.
~Harriet Beecher Stowe

What makes saintliness in my view, as distinguished from ordinary goodness, is a certain quality of magnanimity and greatness of soul that brings life within the circle of the heroic.
~Harriet Beecher Stowe

One would like to be grand and heroic, if one could; but if not, why try at all? One wants to be very something, very great, very heroic; or if not that, then at least very stylish and very fashionable. It is this everlasting mediocrity that bores me.
~Harriet Beecher Stowe

To be really great in little things, to be truly noble and heroic in the insipid details of everyday life, is a virtue so rare as to be worthy of canonization.
~Harriet Beecher Stowe

Perhaps it is impossible for a person who does no good to
do no harm.
~Harriet Beecher Stowe

I am speaking now of the highest duty we owe our
friends, the noblest, the most sacred—
that of keeping their own nobleness, goodness,
pure and incorrupt. . . . If we let our friend become
cold and selfish and exacting without a remonstrance,
we are no true lover, no true friend.
~Harriet Beecher Stowe

Winning has always meant much to me, but winning friends
has meant the most
~Babe Zaharias

Happiness

Susan B. Anthony/Issued 1936

Independence is happiness.
~Susan B. Anthony

Luck? I don't know anything about luck. I've never
banked on it, and I'm afraid of people who do.
Luck to me is something else: Hard work—
and realizing what is opportunity and what isn't.
~Lucille Ball

I would rather regret the things that I have done than the things
that I have not.
~Lucille Ball

Ability is of little account without opportunity.
~Lucille Ball

Growth itself contains the germ of happiness.
~Pearl S. Buck

To eat bread without hope is still slowly starving to death.
~Pearl S. Buck

Order is the shape upon which beauty depends.
~Pearl S. Buck

☜☞

You will never be happier than you expect. To change your happiness, change your expectation.
~Bette Davis

A sure way to lose happiness, I found, is to want it at the expense of everything else.
~Bette Davis

☜☞

Fame is a bee.
It has a song—
It has a sting—
Ah, too, it has a wing.
~Emily Dickinson

Happiness

I'm Nobody! Who are you?
Are you—Nobody—Too?
Then there's a pair of us!
Don't tell! they'd advertise—you know!

How dreary—to be—Somebody!
How public—like a Frog—
To tell one's name—the livelong June—
To an admiring Bog!
~Emily Dickinson

∽୨

No matter what accomplishments you make,
somebody helped you.
~Althea Gibson

∽୨

The most important thing is to enjoy your life—to be happy—
it's all that matters.
~Audrey Hepburn

∽୨

Somebody once said we never know what is enough
until we know what's more than enough.
~Billie Holiday

∽୨

When one door of happiness closes, another opens; but often
we look so long at the closed door that we do not see
the one which has been opened for us.
~Helen Keller

Many persons have a wrong idea of what constitutes true
happiness. It is not attained through self-gratification but
through fidelity to a worthy purpose.
~Helen Keller

Although the world is full of suffering,
it is full also of the overcoming of it.
~Helen Keller

We cannot freely and wisely choose the right way for ourselves
unless we know both good and evil.
~Helen Keller

Keep smiling, because life is a beautiful thing and there's
so much to smile about.
~Marilyn Monroe

She was a girl who knew how to be happy even when she was
sad. And that's important—you know.
~Marilyn Monroe

We are all of us stars, and we deserve to twinkle.
~Marilyn Monroe

They sicken of the calm, who know the storm.
~Dorothy Parker

⁙

I felt my lungs inflate with the onrush of scenery—air,
mountains, trees, people. I thought,
"This is what it is to be happy."
~Sylvia Plath

⁙

Learn to value yourself, which means: fight for your happiness.
~Ayn Rand

A creative man is motivated by the desire to achieve, not by the
desire to beat others.
~Ayn Rand

⁙

Happiness is not a goal...it's a by-product of a life well lived.
~Eleanor Roosevelt

⁙

The longest day must have its close—the gloomiest night will
wear on to a morning. An eternal, inexorable lapse of moments
is ever hurrying the day of the evil to an eternal night, and the
night of the just to an eternal day.
~Harriet Beecher Stowe

If women want any rights they had better take them,
and say nothing about it.
~Harriet Beecher Stowe

In all ranks of life the human heart yearns for the beautiful; and
the beautiful things that God makes are his gift to all alike.
~Harriet Beecher Stowe

Let no one ever come to you without leaving better and happier.
Be the living expression of God's kindness: kindness in your
face, kindness in your eyes, kindness in your smile.
~Mother Teresa

The greatest part of our happiness depends on our dispositions,
not our circumstances.
~Martha Washington

LESSONS

Martha Washington/Issued 1938

If we mean to have heroes, statesmen and philosophers, we
should have learned women.
~Abigail Adams

I'm not afraid of storms, for I'm learning how to sail my ship.
~Louisa May Alcott

One of the things I learned the hard way was that it doesn't pay
to get discouraged. Keeping busy and making optimism a way of
life can restore your faith in yourself.
~Lucille Ball

There are some things you learn best in calm, and some in
storm.
~Willa Cather

You don't make progress by standing on the sidelines, whimpering and complaining. You make progress by implementing ideas.

~Shirley Chisholm

❧

Old age ain't no place for sissies.

~Bette Davis

❧

It isn't where you came from; it's where you're going that counts.

~Ella Fitzgerald

❧

I am sick and tired of being sick and tired.

~Fannie Lou Hamer

There is one thing you have got to learn about our movement. Three people are better than no people.

~Fannie Lou Hamer

❧

If you obey all the rules, you miss all the fun.

~Katharine Hepburn

❧

Lessons

Mama may have
Papa may have
But God bless the child that's got his own.
~Billie Holiday

ᖇ‿ᖆ

There are years that ask questions and years that answer.
~Zora Neale Hurston

ᖇ‿ᖆ

Just remember the world is not a playground but a schoolroom.
Life is not a holiday but an education. One eternal lesson for us all:
to teach us how better we should love.
~Barbara Jordan

ᖇ‿ᖆ

Life is a succession of lessons which must be lived to be
understood.
~Helen Keller

ᖇ‿ᖆ

I always have the best of everything.
~Hattie McDaniel

ᖇ‿ᖆ

I learned the value of hard work by working hard.

~Margaret Mead

❦

Age is not a handicap. Age is nothing but a number.
It is how you use it.

~Ethel L. Payne

❦

Tell me what you'd like to hear me sing.
I'll sing whatever you like, after which I'll take up a collection,
if you don't mind.

~Edith Piaf

❦

If you expect nothing from anybody, you're never disappointed.

~Sylvia Plath

❦

The past is never where you think you left it.

~Katherine Anne Porter

❦

Etiquette requires the presumption of good until the contrary is proved.

~Emily Post

☙

One thing life has taught me: if you are interested, you never have to look for new interests. They come to you. When you are genuinely interested in one thing, it will always lead to something else.

~Eleanor Roosevelt

No one won the last war, and no one will win the next war.

~Eleanor Roosevelt

When will our consciences grow so tender that we will act to prevent human misery rather than avenge it?

~Eleanor Roosevelt

I think that somehow, we learn who we really are and then live with that decision.

~Eleanor Roosevelt

Learn from the mistakes of others. You can't live long enough to make them all yourself.

~Eleanor Roosevelt

Great minds discuss ideas. Average minds discuss events. Small minds discuss people.

~*Eleanor Roosevelt*

If someone betrays you once, it's their fault; if they betray you twice, it's your fault.

~*Eleanor Roosevelt*

I am determined to be cheerful and happy in whatever situation I may find myself. For I have learned that the greater part of our misery or unhappiness is determined not by our circumstance but by our disposition.

~*Martha Washington*

Study the rules so that you won't beat yourself by not knowing something.

~*Babe Zaharias*

Life

Mothers of America/Issued 1934

Life

Poetry is life distilled.
~*Gwendolyn Brooks*

If I can stop one Heart from breaking
I shall not live in vain
If I can ease one Life the Aching
Or cool one Pain

Or help one fainting Robin
Unto his Nest again
I shall not live in Vain.
~*Emily Dickinson*

As one goes through life, one learns that if you don't paddle your
own canoe, you don't move.
~*Katharine Hepburn*

Everybody needs somebody.
~*Mahalia Jackson*

If you are politically inclined, you may be President of the United States. All my growth and development led me to believe that if you really do the right thing, and if you play by the rules, and if you've got good enough, solid judgment and common sense, that you're going to be able to do whatever you want to do with your life.
~Barbara Jordan

Life is either a daring adventure or nothing.
~Helen Keller

When we do the best that we can,
we never know what miracle is wrought in our life,
or in the life of another.
~Helen Keller

I wouldn't change one thing about my professional life, and I make it a point not to dwell on my mistakes.
~Ethel Merman

Life's under no obligation to give us what we expect.
~Margaret Mitchell

You never know what life is like, until you have lived it.
~Marilyn Monroe

∽

Life is what we make it, always has been, always will be.
~Grandma Moses

∽

I've been absolutely terrified every moment of my life and I've never let it keep me from doing a single thing that I wanted to do.
~Georgia O'Keeffe

Where I was born and where and how I have lived is unimportant. It is what I have done with where I have been that should be of interest.
~Georgia O'Keeffe

∽

Each person must live their life as a model for others.
~Rosa Parks

∽

Do not stop thinking of life as an adventure. You have no security unless you can live bravely, excitingly, imaginatively; unless you can choose a challenge instead of competence.
~Eleanor Roosevelt

Many people will walk in and out of your life, but only true
friends will leave footprints in your heart.
~Eleanor Roosevelt

Life is what you make it. Always has been, always will be.
~Eleanor Roosevelt

In the long run, we shape our lives, and we shape ourselves.
The process never ends until we die. And the choices
we make are ultimately our own responsibility.
~Eleanor Roosevelt

The purpose of life is to live it, to taste experience to the utmost,
to reach out eagerly and without fear for newer
and richer experience.
~Eleanor Roosevelt

Life was meant to be lived, and curiosity must be kept alive.
One must never, for whatever reason, turn his back on life.
~Eleanor Roosevelt

Never mistake knowledge for wisdom. One helps you make a
living; the other helps you make a life.
~Eleanor Roosevelt

A mature person is one who does not think only in absolutes,
who is able to be objective even when deeply stirred
emotionally, who has learned that there is both good and bad in
all people and in all things, and who walks humbly and deals
charitably with the circumstances of life, knowing that in this
world no one is all knowing and therefore all of us need both
love and charity.
~Eleanor Roosevelt

Life

Winning is great, sure, but if you are really going to do something in life, the secret is learning how to lose. Nobody goes undefeated all the time. If you can pick up after a crushing defeat, and go on to win again, you are going to be a champion someday.

~Wilma Rudolph

Trouble is part of your life—if you don't share it, you don't give the person who loves you a chance to love you enough.

~Dinah Shore

The heyday of woman's life is the shady side of fifty.

~Elizabeth Cady Stanton

Profound joy of the heart is like a magnet that indicates the path of life. One has to follow it, even though one enters into a way full of difficulties.

~Mother Teresa

It's not how much you do, but how much love you put into what you do that counts.

~Mother Teresa

There is no royal flower-strewn path to success. And if there is,
I have not found it for if I have accomplished anything in life
it is because I have been willing to work hard.

~Madam C J. Walker

Life is always either a tightrope or a feather bed.
Give me the tightrope.

~Edith Wharton

The world is wide, and I will not waste my life in friction
when it could be turned into momentum.

~Frances E. Willard

You have to play by the rules of golf just as you have to live
by the rules of life. There's no other way.

~Babe Zaharias

Love

Grandma Moses/Issued 1969

Love

Love dies only when growth stops.
~Pearl S. Buck

Where there is great love, there are always miracles.
~Willa Cather

Just don't give up trying to do what you really want to do.
Where there is love and inspiration, I don't think you can go
wrong.
~Ella Fitzgerald

If I'm honest I have to tell you I still read fairy tales and I like
them best of all.
~Audrey Hepburn

Love has nothing to do with what you are expecting to get—only with what you are expecting to give—which is everything.
~*Katharine Hepburn*

༄

Love is like a faucet, it turns off and on.
~*Billie Holiday*

༄

Love is like a beautiful flower which I may not touch, but whose fragrance makes the garden a place of delight just the same.
~*Helen Keller*

What we have once enjoyed we can never lose. All that we love deeply becomes a part of us.
~*Helen Keller*

༄

The heart that gives, gathers.
~*Marianne Moore*

༄

I look back on my life like a good day's work, it was done and I feel satisfied with it. I was happy and contented, I knew nothing better and made the best out of what life offered. And life is what we make it, always has been, always will be.
~*Grandma Moses*

༄

Love

Four be the things I'd have been better without: Love, curiosity, freckles and doubt.
~*Dorothy Parker*

༄

Love must be learned and learned again; There is no end.
~*Katherine Anne Porter*

༄

You wouldn't worry so much about what others think of you if you realized how seldom they do.
~*Eleanor Roosevelt*

We are afraid to care too much, for fear that the other person does not care at all.
~*Eleanor Roosevelt*

The reason that fiction is more interesting than any other form of literature, to those who really like to study people, is that in fiction the author can really tell the truth without humiliating himself.
~*Eleanor Roosevelt*

I think, at a child's birth, if a mother could ask a fairy godmother to endow it with the most useful gift, that gift would be curiosity.
~*Eleanor Roosevelt*

To handle yourself, use your head; to handle others,
use your heart.
~Eleanor Roosevelt

❧

The unthankful heart discovers no mercies; but the thankful
heart will find, in every hour, some heavenly blessings.
~Harriet Beecher Stowe

I would not attack the faith of a heathen without being sure I had
a better one to put in its place.
~Harriet Beecher Stowe

A little reflection will enable any person to detect in himself that
setness in trifles which is the result of the unwatched instinct of
self-will and to establish over himself a jealous guardianship.
~Harriet Beecher Stowe

In all ranks of life the human heart yearns for the beautiful;
and the beautiful things that God makes are his gift to all alike.
~Harriet Beecher Stowe

Any mind that is capable of real sorrow is capable of good.
~Harriet Beecher Stowe

❧

Joy is a net of love by which you can catch souls. A joyful heart
is the inevitable result of a heart burning with love.
~Mother Teresa

Love

Not all of us can do great things. But we can do small things with great love.

~Mother Teresa

Being unwanted, unloved, uncared for, forgotten by everybody, I think that is a much greater hunger, a much greater poverty than the person who has nothing to eat.

~Mother Teresa

Do not think that love in order to be genuine has to be extraordinary. What we need is to love without getting tired.

~Mother Teresa

I have found the paradox, that if you love until it hurts, there can be no more hurt, only more love.

~Mother Teresa

If you can't feed a hundred people, then just feed one.

~Mother Teresa

If you judge people, you have no time to love them.

~Mother Teresa

Love is a fruit in season at all times, and within reach of every hand.

~Mother Teresa

Peace begins with a smile.

~Mother Teresa

Possibility

Emily Dickinson/Issued August 1971

The good we secure for ourselves is precarious and uncertain until it is secured for all of us and incorporated into our common life.
~Jane Addams

Nothing could be worse than the fear that one had given up too soon, and left one unexpended effort that might have saved the world.
~Jane Addams

I have an almost complete disregard of precedent, and a faith in the possibility of something better. It irritates me to be told how things have always been done. I defy the tyranny of precedent. I go for anything new that might improve the past.
~Clara Barton

A man's indebtedness is not virtue; his repayment is. Virtue begins when he dedicates himself actively to the job of gratitude.
~Ruth Benedict

All things are possible until they are proved impossible—and
even the impossible may only be so, as of now.
~Pearl S. Buck

෴

I think that if you shake the tree, you ought to be around when
the fruit falls to pick it up.
~Mary Cassatt

෴

What I can do—I will—
Though it be little as a Daffodil—
That I cannot—must be
Unknown to possibility—
~Emily Dickinson

I dwell in Possibility—
A fairer House than Prose—
More numerous of Windows—
Superior—for Doors—
~Emily Dickinson

Anger as soon as fed is dead—
'Tis starving makes it fat—
~Emily Dickinson

Possibility

Hope is a strange invention—
A Patent of the Heart—
In unremitting action
Yet never wearing out—
~Emily Dickinson

The Possible's slow fuse is lit
By the Imagination.
~Emily Dickinson

☙

Some of us have great runways already built for us.
If you have one, take OFF! But if you don't have one,
realize it is your responsibility to grab a shovel and
build one for yourself and for those who will follow after you.
~Amelia Earhart

☙

I never said, "I want to be alone." I only said "I want to be *let*
alone!" There is all the difference.
~Greta Garbo

☙

Always be a first rate version of yourself and not a second rate
version of someone else.
~Judy Garland

I've always taken *The Wizard of Oz* very seriously, you know. I believe in the idea of the rainbow. And I've spent my entire life trying to get over it.
~Judy Garland

❦

It's okay to have butterflies…but we have to teach them to fly in formation.
~Katharine Hepburn

❦

Keep your face to the sun and you will never see the shadows.
~Helen Keller

Be of good cheer. Do not think of today's failures, but of the success that may come tomorrow. You have set yourselves a difficult task, but you will succeed if you persevere; and you will find a joy in overcoming obstacles. Remember, no effort that we make to attain something beautiful is ever lost.
~Helen Keller

❦

Forgive all who have offended you, not for them, but for yourself.
~Harriet Nelson

❦

Possibility

The cure for boredom is curiosity.
There is no cure for curiosity.
~Dorothy Parker

I started my life with a single absolute: that the world was mine to shape in the image of my highest values and never to be given up to a lesser standard, no matter how long or hard the struggle.
~Ayn Rand

If you don't know, the thing to do is not to get scared, but to learn.
~Ayn Rand

You can avoid reality, but you cannot avoid the consequences of avoiding reality.
~Ayn Rand

You can often change your circumstances by changing your attitude.
~Eleanor Roosevelt

Imagination is the only key to the future. Without it none exists—with it all things are possible.
~Ida Tarbell

A mind which really lays hold of a subject is not easily detached from it.
~Ida Tarbell

I can do things you cannot, you can do things I cannot; together we can do great things.
~Mother Teresa

Yesterday is gone. Tomorrow has not yet come. We have only today. Let us begin.
~Mother Teresa

I knew right away that it was a gorgeous idea.
~Lila Wallace

The way to right wrongs is to turn the light of truth upon them.
~Ida B. Wells

Service

Service Women/Issued 1952

Remember the Ladies, and be more generous and favorable to
them than your ancestors.
~Abigail Adams

Action is indeed the sole medium of expression for ethics.
~Jane Addams

To serve is beautiful, but only if it is done with joy and a whole
heart and a free mind.
~Pearl S. Buck

The person who tries to live alone will not succeed as a human
being. His heart withers if it does not answer another heart. His
mind shrinks away if he hears only the echoes of his own
thoughts and finds no other inspiration
~Pearl S. Buck

Many people lose the small joys in the hope for the big
happiness.
~Pearl S. Buck

∽⊘

We trust, in plumed procession
For such, the Angels go—
Rank after Rank, with even feet—
And Uniforms of Snow.
~Emily Dickinson

Luck is not chance—
It's Toil—
Fortune's expensive smile
Is earned—
~Emily Dickinson

We never know how high we are—
Till we are called to rise
~Emily Dickinson

This is my letter to the World
That never wrote to Me—
The simple News that Nature told—
With tender Majesty

Her Message is committed
To Hands I cannot see—
For love of Her—Sweet—countrymen—
Judge tenderly—of Me
~Emily Dickinson

Service

I know not how to thank you…To give delight is hallowed—
perhaps the toil of angels, whose avocations are concealed.

~Emily Dickinson

The most difficult thing is the decision to act,
the rest is merely tenacity.

~Amelia Earhart

Nothing is impossible, the word itself says, "I'm possible!"

~Audrey Hepburn

As you grow older, you will discover that you have two hands,
one for helping yourself, the other for helping others.

~Audrey Hepburn

I love people who make me laugh. I honestly think it's the thing
I like most, to laugh. It cures a multitude of ills. It's probably the
most important thing in a person.

~Audrey Hepburn

I am confirmed in my division of human energies.
Ambitious people climb, but faithful people build.

~Julia Ward Howe

Faith and prayer are the vitamins of the soul; man cannot live in health without them.
~*Mahalia Jackson*

∽

Many people have the wrong idea of what constitutes true happiness. It is not attained through self gratification, but through fidelity to a worthy cause.
~*Helen Keller*

There is no king who has not had a slave among his ancestors, and no slave who has not had a king among his.
~*Helen Keller*

You will succeed if you persevere; and you will find joy in overcoming obstacles.
~*Helen Keller*

∽

A badge is a symbol that you have done the thing it stands for often enough, thoroughly enough, and well enough to BE PREPARED to give service in it.
~*Juliette Gordon Low*

∽

Service

We are continually faced with great opportunities which are brilliantly disguised as unsolvable problems.

~Margaret Mead

ᕙᕗ

You're not free
until you've been made captive by
supreme belief.

~Marianne Moore

ᕙᕗ

The ladder of success is best climbed by stepping on the rungs of opportunity.

~Ayn Rand

The question isn't who is going to let me;
it's who is going to stop me.

~Ayn Rand

ᕙᕗ

No one can make you feel inferior without your consent.

~Eleanor Roosevelt

The giving of love is an education in itself.

~Eleanor Roosevelt

ᕙᕗ

Be faithful in small things because it is in them that
your strength lies. .
~Mother Teresa

If we have no peace, it is because we have forgotten that we
belong to each other.
~Mother Teresa

I am not sure exactly what heaven will be like, but I know that
when we die and it comes time for God to judge us, he will not
ask, "How many good things have you done in your life?" rather
he will ask, "How much love did you put into what you did?"
~Mother Teresa

It is the mind that makes the body.
~Sojourner Truth

Truth is powerful and it prevails.
~Sojourner Truth

Strength

Progress of Women/Issued 1948

Great necessities call out great virtues.
~Abigail Adams

I believe in prayer. It's the best way we have to draw strength
from heaven.
~Josephine Baker

I'm not funny. What I am is brave.
~Lucille Ball

If you want something done, ask a busy person to do it.
The more things you do, the more you can do.
~Lucille Ball

In life, all good things come hard, but wisdom is the hardest to
come by.
~Lucille Ball

You grow up the day you have your first real laugh at yourself.

~Ethel Barrymore

❦

Faith is the first factor in a life devoted to service. Without it, nothing is possible. With it, nothing is impossible.

~Mary McLeod Bethune

❦

Ports are necessities, like postage stamps or soap, but they seldom seem to care what impressions they make.

~Elizabeth Bishop

❦

Great thoughts speak only to the thoughtful mind, but great actions speak to all mankind.

~Emily P. Bissell

❦

Our bodies can be mobilized by law and police and men with guns, if necessary—but where shall we find that which will make us believe in what we must do, so that we can fight through to victory?

~Pearl S. Buck

Strength

There is, of course a difference between what one seizes and
what one really possesses.

~Pearl S. Buck

∞

I would never have gone anywhere if it hadn't been for Mother's
faith and support.

~Patsy Cline

∞

This became a credo of mine...attempt the impossible in order to
improve your work.

~Bette Davis

To fulfill a dream, to be allowed to sweat over lonely labor, to be
given a chance to create, is the meat and potatoes of life.
The money is the gravy.

~Bette Davis

∞

Assent—and you are sane—
Demur—you're straightway dangerous—
And handled with a Chain—

~Emily Dickinson

Faith—is the Pierless Bridge
Supporting what We see
Unto the Scene that We do not—
Too slender for the eye
~Emily Dickinson

ᕔᕒ

You were once wild here. Don't let them tame you.
~Isadora Duncan

ᕔᕒ

The most effective way to do it, is to do it.
~Amelia Earhart

ᕔᕒ

We move about the stage without bumping into the furniture.
~Lynn Fontanne

ᕔᕒ

The best thing to hold onto in life is each other.
~Audrey Hepburn

ᕔᕒ

Avoiding danger is no safer in the long run than outright
exposure. The fearful are caught as often as the bold.
~Helen Keller

To keep our faces toward change and behave like free spirits in the presence of fate is strength undefeatable.

~Helen Keller

෧෴ඁ

If you know you're right, you don't care. You know that sooner or later, it will come out in the wash.

~Barbara McClintock

෧෴ඁ

I'd rather die tomorrow than live a hundred years without knowing you.

~Pocahontas

෧෴ඁ

With the new day comes new strength and new thoughts.

~Eleanor Roosevelt

You have to accept whatever comes, and the only important thing is that you meet it with the best you have to give.

~Eleanor Roosevelt

Never allow a person to tell you no who doesn't have the power to say yes.

~Eleanor Roosevelt

A woman is like a tea bag; you never know how strong it is until it's in hot water.

~Eleanor Roosevelt

I would fight for my liberty so long as my strength lasted, and if the time came for me to go, the Lord would let them take me.

~Harriet Tubman

For God and Home and Every Land.
~Frances E. Willard

Work

International Women's Year/Issued 1975

Nothing can be worse than the fear that one had given up too soon and left one unexpended effort which might have saved the world.

~Jane Addams

The essence of immorality is the tendency to make an exception of myself.

~Jane Addams

Try not to do too many things at once. Know what you want, the number one thing today and tomorrow. Persevere and get it done.

~Gracie Allen

If you want to catch more fish, use more hooks.

~Gracie Allen

Forget conventionalisms; forget what the world thinks of you stepping out of your place; think your best thoughts, speak your best words, work your best works, looking to your own conscience for approval.
~Susan B. Anthony

Nobody, but nobody, is going to stop breathing on me.
~Virginia Apgar

Energy rightly applied and directed will accomplish anything.
~Nellie Bly

The easiest thing is to do, the next easiest is to write, and the hardest is to think.
~Mary Breckinridge

There are many ways of breaking a heart. Stories were full of hearts broken by love, but what really broke a heart was taking away its dream—whatever that dream might be.
~Pearl S. Buck

The secret of joy in work is contained in one word—excellence.
To know how to do something well is to enjoy it.
~Pearl S. Buck

❧

Women are essentially practical because they've always had to
be. From the dawn of time it's been our job to see that both ends
meet.
~Hattie W. Caraway

❧

Those who start out as outcasts can wind up as being part of the
system.
~Patricia Roberts Harris

❧

If you rest, you rust.
~Helen Hayes

❧

I know that someday I will die, but I will never retire.
~Margaret Mead

❧

Burdens are for shoulders strong enough to carry them.
~Margaret Mitchell

❧

Imperfection is beauty, madness is genius and it's better to be absolutely ridiculous than absolutely boring.
~Marilyn Monroe

Wanting to be someone else is a waste of the person you are.
~Marilyn Monroe

Aim at a high mark and you'll hit it. No, not the first time, nor the second time. Maybe not the third. But keep on aiming and keep on shooting for only practice will make you perfect.
~Annie Oakley

If you take a flower in your hand and really look at it, it's your world for a moment.
~Georgia O'Keeffe

Work is always an antidote to depression.
~Eleanor Roosevelt

What could we accomplish if we knew we could not fail?
~Eleanor Roosevelt

Work

It is not fair to ask of others what you are not willing to do yourself.

~Eleanor Roosevelt

༄

The right way is not always the popular and easy way. Standing for right when it is unpopular is a true test of moral character.

~Margaret Chase Smith

I always try to think before I talk.

~Margaret Chase Smith

༄

We hold these truths to be self-evident: that all men and women are created equal.

~Elizabeth Cady Stanton

༄

When you get into a tight place and everything goes against you, till it seems as though you could not hang on a minute longer, never give up then, for that is just the place and time that the tide will turn.

~Harriet Beecher Stowe

༄

Keep on beginning and failing. Each time you fail, start all over again, and you will grow stronger until you have accomplished a purpose — not the one you began with perhaps, but one you'll be glad to remember.

~Anne Sullivan

I had to make my own living and my own opportunity. But I made it! Don't sit down and wait for the opportunities to come. Get up and make them.

~Madam C.J. Walker

I got my start by giving myself a start.

~Madam C.J. Walker

Perseverance is my motto.

~Madam C.J. Walker

The formula for success is simple: practice and concentration then more practice and more concentration.

~Babe Zaharias

Biographical Index

Adams, Abigail: 1744–1818, American wife of John Adams, the first Vice President, and second President, of the United States, Former First Lady of the United States, and the mother of John Quincy Adams, the sixth President of the United States.

Addams, Jane: 1860–1935, American pioneer, social worker, public philosopher, sociologist, author, and leader in women's suffrage, issues of concern to mothers including the needs of children and public health, and world peace. She was one of the most prominent reformers of the Progressive Era.

Alcott, Louisa May: 1832–1888, American novelist best known as the author of the novel *Little Women*.

Allen, Gracie: 1895–1964, American comedienne who became internationally famous with comic partner and husband George Burns.

Anderson, Marian: 1897–1993, African-American contralto and one of the most celebrated singers of the twentieth century.

Anthony, Susan B.: 1820–1906, American social reformer who played a pivotal role in the women's suffrage movement and was committed to social equality. She became the New York state agent for the American Anti-Slavery Society.

Apgar, Virginia: 1909–1974, American obstetrical anesthesiologist and leader in the fields of anesthesiology and teratology. She is best known as the developer of the Apgar score which tests the health of newborn children.

Baker, Ella: 1903–1986, African-American civil rights and human rights activist. She has been called "One of the most important African-American leaders of the twentieth century and perhaps the most influential woman in the civil rights movement."

Baker, Josephine: 1906–1975, American-born French dancer, singer, and actress who came to be known in various circles as the "Black Pearl," "Bronze Venus" and even the "Creole Goddess." She was the first African-American woman to star in a major   motion picture, *Zouzou* (1934).

Ball, Lucille: 1911–1989, American comedian, model, film and television actress and studio executive. She was star of the sitcoms *I Love Lucy*, *The Lucy–Desi Comedy Hour*, *The Lucy Show*, *Here's Lucy*, and *Life with Lucy*.

Barrymore, Ethel: 1879–1959, American actress.

Barton, Clara: 1821–1912, American nurse, teacher, patent clerk, and humanitarian. She founded the American Red Cross.

Bates, Daisy Gatson: 1914–1999, African-American civil rights activist, publisher, journalist, and lecturer.

Bates, Katherine Lee: 1859–1929, American songwriter. She is remembered as the author of the words to the anthem "America the Beautiful."

Benedict, Ruth: 1887–1948, American anthropologist.

Bethune, Mary McLeod: 1875–1955, African-American educator and civil rights leader also known as "The First Lady of The Struggle."

Bishop, Elizabeth: 1911–1979, American poet and short-story writer. She was the Poet Laureate of the United States from 1949 to 1950. In 1956, she won the Pulitzer Prize for Poetry, in 1970 she was the National Book Award winner, and in 1976 she was the recipient of the Neustadt International Prize for Literature.

Bissell, Emily: 1861–1948, American social worker and activist, best remembered for introducing Christmas Seals to the United States.

Blackwell, Elizabeth: 1821–1910, British-American and was the first woman to receive a medical degree in the United States, as well as the first woman on the UK Medical Register. She was the first openly identified woman to graduate from medical school and a pioneer in promoting the education of women in medicine in the United States.

Bly, Nellie: 1864–1922, American journalist.

Breckinridge, Mary: 1881–1965, American nurse-midwife and the founder of the Frontier Nursing Service.

Brice, Fanny: 1891–1951, American comedian, singer, theater and film actress who is also known as the creator and star of the top-rated radio comedy series, *The Baby Snooks Show*.

Brooks, Gwendolyn: 1917–2000, African-American poet. She won the Pulitzer Prize for Poetry in 1950 and was appointed Poet Laureate of Illinois in 1968 and Poet Laureate Consultant in Poetry to the Library of Congress in 1985.

Buck, Pearl S.: 1892–1973, American writer and novelist. Her novel *The Good Earth* was the best-selling fiction book in the U.S. in 1931 and 1932 and she won the Pulitzer Prize in 1932. In 1938, she was awarded the Nobel Prize in Literature.

Caraway, Hattie, W.: 1878–1950, American politician and the first woman elected to serve a full term as a United States Senator. Senator Caraway represented Arkansas.

Carson, Rachel: 1907–1964, American marine biologist and conservationist. Her book *Silent Spring* and other writings are credited with advancing the global environmental movement and her widely praised 1951 bestseller *The Sea Around Us* won a U.S. National Book Award.

Cassatt, Mary: 1844–1926, American painter and printmaker. Cassatt exhibited among the Impressionists and often created images of the social and private lives of women, with particular emphasis on the intimate bonds between mothers and children.

Cather, Willa: 1873–1947, American author who achieved recognition for her novels of frontier life on the Great Plains, in works such as *O Pioneers!*, *My Ántonia*, and *The Song of the Lark*. In 1923 she was awarded the Pulitzer Prize for *One of Ours* (1922), a novel set during World War I.

Chisholm, Shirley: 1924–2005, African-American politician, educator, and author. She was the first African-American woman elected to Congress.

Cline, Patsy: 1932–1963, American country music singer.

Cunningham, Imogen: 1883–1976, American photographer known for her botanical photography, nudes, and industrial landscapes.

Davis, Bette: 1908–1989, American actress of film, television and theater. She is also known as "The First Lady of American Cinema."

de Mille, Agnes: 1905–1933, American dancer and choreographer.

Dickinson, Emily: 1830–1886, American poet who wrote more than 1,700 poems and numerous letters.

Duncan, Isadora: 1877–1927, American dancer.

Earhart, Amelia: 1897–1937, American aviation pioneer and author. She was the first female aviator to fly solo across the Atlantic Ocean.

Fitzgerald, Ella: 1917–1996, African-American jazz vocalist. She is also known as the "First Lady of Song" and the "Queen of Jazz."

Fontanne, Lynn: 1887–1983, British-born American-based actress.

Garbo, Greta: 1905–1990, Swedish film actress and an international star and icon during Hollywood's silent and classic periods.

Garland, Judy: 1922–1969, American actress, singer, and vaudevillian. Described by Fred Astaire as "the greatest entertainer who ever lived."

Gellhorn, Martha: 1908–1998, American novelist, travel writer, and journalist, considered by the London *Daily Telegraph*, among others, to be one of the greatest war correspondents of the 20th century.

Gibson, Althea: 1927–2003, African-American tennis player and professional golfer, and the first black athlete of either gender to cross the color line of international tennis.

Graham, Martha: 1894–1991, American modern dancer and choreographer.

Hamer, Fannie Lou: 1917–1977, African-American voting rights activist and civil rights leader.

Harris, Patricia Roberts: 1924–1985, African-American politician. She served in the administration of President Jimmy Carter as United States Secretary of Housing and Urban Development, and United States Secretary of Health, Education, and Welfare (which was renamed the Secretary of Health and Human Services during her tenure). She was the first African-American woman to serve in the United States Cabinet, and the first to enter the line of succession to the Presidency.

Hayes, Helen: 1900–1993, American actress. She was also known as the "First Lady of the American Theatre" and is one of a select group who has won an Emmy, a Grammy, an Oscar, and a Tony Award.

Hepburn, Audrey: 1929–1993, British actress, film and fashion icon, and humanitarian.

Hepburn, Katharine: 1907–2003, American actress of film, stage, and television.

Hobby, Oveta Culp: 1905–1995, American politician. She was the first secretary of the U.S. Department of Health, Education and Welfare and the first commanding officer of the Women's Army Corps.

Holiday, Billie: 1915–1959, African-American jazz singer and songwriter. She was nicknamed "Lady Day."

Howe, Julia Ward: 1819–1910, American abolitionist, social activist, poet, and the author of "The Battle Hymn of the Republic."

Hurston, Zora Neale: 1891–1960, African-American folklorist, anthropologist, and author.

Isabella I of Castile: 1451–1504, Spanish Queen. She and her husband, Ferdinand II of Aragon, are known for supporting and financing Christopher Columbus' 1492 voyage that led to the opening of the "New World."

Jackson, Mahalia: 1911–1972, African-American gospel singer. She was also known as "The Queen of Gospel."

Johnson, "Lady Bird": 1912–2007, American wife and First Lady of the United States during the presidency of her husband, Lyndon B. Johnson.

Jordan, Barbara: 1936–1996, African-American politician and a leader of the Civil Rights movement.

Kahlo, Frida: 1907–1954, Mexican painter who is best known for her self-portraits.

Käsebier, Gertrude: 1852–1934, American photographer. She was known for her evocative images of motherhood, her powerful portraits of Native Americans and her promotion of photography as a career for women.

Keller, Helen: 1880-1968, American author, lecturer, and activist.

Kelly, Grace: 1929–1982, American film actress.

Levertov, Denise: 1923–1997, British-born American poet.

Lockwood, Belva Ann: 1830–1917, American attorney, politician, educator, and author.

Low, Juliette Gordon: 1860–1927, American founder of Girl Scouts of the USA.

Ludington, Sybil: 1761–1839, American heroine of the American Revolutionary War. She is famous for her night ride on April 26, 1777 to alert American colonial forces to the approach of the British.

Lyon, Mary: 1797–1849, American pioneer in women's education. She established both the Wheaton Female Seminary in Norton, Massachusetts, (now Wheaton College) and Mount Holyoke Female Seminary (now Mount Holyoke College).

Madison, Dolley: 1768–1849, American wife of James Madison, President of the United States from 1809 to 1817. She did much to define the role of the President's spouse, known only much later by the title First Lady.

McClintock, Barbara: 1902–1992, American scientist.

McDaniel, Hattie: 1895–1952, African-American actress. She was the first African-American to be nominated and to win an Academy Award. She won the award for Best Supporting Actress for her role of Mammy in *Gone with the Wind* (1939).

Mead, Margaret: 1901–1978, American cultural anthropologist, author, and speaker.

Merman, Ethel: 1908–1984, American actress and singer.

Millay, Edna St. Vincent: 1892–1950, American lyrical poet and playwright. She received the Pulitzer Prize for Poetry in 1923.

Mitchell, Margaret: 1900–1949, American author and journalist. Her American Civil War-era novel, *Gone with the Wind* won the National Book Award for Most Distinguished Novel of 1936 and the Pulitzer Prize for Fiction in 1937.

Monroe, Marilyn: 1926–1962, American actress, model, and singer.

Moore, Marianne: 1887–1972, American Modernist poet and writer.

Moses, Anna Mary Robertson ("Grandma Moses"): 1860–1961, American folk artist.

Mott, Lucretia: 1793–1880, American Quaker, abolitionist, a women's rights activist, and a social reformer.

Nelson, Harriet: 1909–1994, American singer and actress. She is best known for her role on the long-running sitcom *The Adventures of Ozzie and Harriet*.

Nevelson, Louise: 1899–1988, Russian-born American sculptor known for her monumental, monochromatic, wooden wall pieces and outdoor sculptures.

Oakley, Annie: 1860–1926, American sharpshooter and exhibition shooter also known as "Little Sure Shot."

O'Keeffe, Georgia: 1887–1986, American artist.

Parker, Dorothy: 1893–1967, American poet, short story writer, critic, and satirist.

Parks, Rosa: 1913–2005, African-American civil rights activist, whom the United States Congress called "the first lady of civil rights" and "the mother of the freedom movement."

Paul, Alice: 1885–1977, African-American suffragist, feminist, and women's rights activist.

Payne, Ethel L.: 1911–1991, African-American journalist. She was also known as the "First Lady of the Black Press."

Piaf, Edith: 1915–1963, French singer.

Plath, Sylvia: 1932–1963, American poet, novelist, and short-story writer.

Pocahontas: 1595–1617, Virginia Indian notable for her association with the colonial settlement at Jamestown, Virginia.

Porter, Katherine Anne: 1890–1980, American journalist, essayist, short story writer, novelist, and political activist. Her 1962 novel *Ship of Fools* won the Pulitzer Prize.

Post, Emily: 1872–1960, American author famous for writing about etiquette.

Rand, Ayn: 1905–1982, American novelist, philosopher, playwright, and screenwriter. She is known for her two best-selling novels, *The Fountainhead* and *Atlas Shrugged*, and for developing a philosophical system she called Objectivism.

Roosevelt, Eleanor: 1884–1962, American writer and First Lady of the United States.

Ross, Betsy: 1752–1836, American seamstress who is widely credited with making the first American flag.

Rudolf, Wilma: 1940–1994, African-American athlete and an Olympic champion. In the 1960 Summer Olympics in Rome, she became the first American woman to win three gold medals in track and field during a single Olympic Games and was considered the fastest woman in the world in the 1960s.

Shore, Dinah: 1916–1994, American singer, actress, and television personality.

Smith, Margaret Chase: 1897–1995, American politician.

Stanton, Elizabeth Cady: 1815–1902, American social activist, abolitionist, and leading figure of the early women's rights movement.

Stowe, Harriet Beecher: 1811–1896, American abolitionist and author known for her novel *Uncle Tom's Cabin*.

Sullivan, Anne: 1866–1936, American teacher best known as the instructor and lifelong companion of Helen Keller.

Tarbell, Ida M.: 1857–1944, American teacher, author and journalist.

Teresa, Mother: 1910–1997, Albanian nun.

Truth, Sojourner: 1797–1883, African-American abolitionist and women's rights activist.

Tubman, Harriet: 1820–1913, African-American abolitionist, humanitarian, and Union spy during the American Civil War.

Walker, Madam C.J.: 1867–1919, African-American entrepreneur and philanthropist. She is regarded as the first female self-made millionaire in America by developing and marketing beauty and hair products for black women under the company she founded, Madam C.J. Walker Manufacturing Company.

Wallace, Lila Acheson: 1889–1984, United States magazine publisher.

Washington, Martha: 1731–1802, American and the wife of George Washington, the first president of the United States. Although the title was not coined until after her death, Martha Washington is considered to be the first First Lady of the United States.

Wells, Ida B.: 1862–1931, African-American journalist, newspaper editor, suffragist, sociologist, and an early leader in the civil rights movement.

Wharton, Edith: 1862–1937, American novelist, short story writer, and designer. Her book *The Age of Innocence* (1920) won the 1921 Pulitzer Prize for literature, making Wharton the first woman to win the award.

Willard, Frances E.: 1839–1898, American educator, temperance reformer, and women's suffragist. Her influence was instrumental in the passage of the Eighteenth (Prohibition) and Nineteenth (Women Suffrage) Amendments to the United States Constitution.

Zaharias, Mildred Didrikson ("Babe"): 1911–1956, American athlete who achieved outstanding success in golf, basketball, and track and field.

Jackson, Mahalia: 59, 86
Johnson, "Lady Bird": 30
Jordan, Barbara: 53, 60

Kahlo, Frida: 20
Käsebier, Gertrude: 20
Keller, Helen: 12, 21, 37, 46, 53, 60, 68, 78, 86, 94, 95
Kelly, Grace: 30

Levertov, Denise: 21
Lockwood, Belva Ann: 21
Low, Juliette Gordon: 21, 30, 37, 86
Ludington, Sybil: 21
Lyon, Mary: 30

Madison, Dolley: 30
McClintock, Barbara: 22, 30, 95
McDaniel, Hattie: 37, 53
Mead, Margaret: 31, 54, 87, 101
Merman, Ethel: 60
Millay, Edna St. Vincent: 12, 22, 38
Mitchell, Margaret: 22, 60, 101
Monroe, Marilyn: 31, 46, 61, 102
Moore, Marianne: 12, 68, 87
Moses, Anna Mary Robertson ("Grandma Moses"): 22, 61, 68
Mott, Lucretia: 12

Nelson, Harriet: 78
Nevelson, Louise: 31

Oakley, Annie: 102
O'Keeffe, Georgia: 22, 61, 102

Parker, Dorothy: 12, 47, 69, 79
Parks, Rosa: 22, 31, 61

About the Editor

Kathleen Welton is the editor and publisher of *The Little Quote Books* series including *The Little Book of Gratitude Quotes*, *The Little Book of Horse Quotes*, *The Little Book of Humorous Quotes*, *The Little Book of Quotes by Women*, and *The Little Book of Success Quotes*.

In addition, she is co-editor of *100 Essential Modern Poems by Women with Joseph Parisi* and co-author of *Poetry For Beginners with Margaret Chapman*.

During her career as an award-winning editor and publisher, she has had the opportunity to serve as Director of Book Publishing for the American Bar Association, Vice President & Publisher for IDG Books, Vice President & Publisher for Dearborn Trade, and Senior Editor for Dow Jones-Irwin.

She earned a BA degree in English from Stanford University and is a graduate of the Stanford Publishing Course.